Fr　　　ﾞ

Mother Magdalen

1832-1900

Servant of God

by
Sr Eithne Leonard

All booklets are published thanks to the
generous support of the members of the
Catholic Truth Society

CATHOLIC TRUTH SOCIETY
PUBLISHERS TO THE HOLY SEE

Contents

Victorian Childhood

There were nine children already in the Rectory of Stoke Rochford Parish Lincolnshire, England, when, on 20th January 1832 Frances Margaret Taylor was born. Her father, Henry Taylor, an Oxford graduate, had been curate of St Mary Abbots, Kensington, as had his father before him. Her mother, Louisa Jones, a Londoner and daughter of prosperous merchants, was, like her husband, a fervent Christian and a loyal member of the Church of England. Having nine children, all healthy, seemed enough for Louisa. Understandably, she was anxious about adding a tenth child, and in 1832 that was a very real risk for mother and child. Most families in the 1800s would have known the grief of the loss of one or more children. She thanked God for the safe arrival of this little girl. Before her first birthday, however, Frances was to lose her ten-year-old sister, Harriet. Frances was warmly welcomed by the lively family of three brothers and six sisters, all less than fifteen years old.

From country parsonage to city slums

Laughter and the ability to give joy characterised Frances throughout life, and like all youngest children, her

siblings played their part in her early growth and education. Formal lessons in the rectory were provided by an aunt, and she was a quick learner. Her country home meant a childhood lived in healthy fresh air with plain, wholesome food. 'We were out in snow, rain and wind; wore simple clothing; were seldom ill and were not over-burdened with lessons.'

The family Sundays were kept faithfully attending services, at which Rev. Henry Taylor read and eloquently explained the Scriptures and later Evensong was sung together. The girls had lovely singing voices and this devotional end to the sabbath day was a joy shared by all members of the family and friends and domestic helpers. In her thirties, visiting a cathedral while on her journey to Poland, Frances wrote: 'The music not quite so bad; really bad music in Church is, to me, absolute pain.'

Baptisms especially attracted Frances; as a child she would never miss a Baptism service in the Parish Church and loved to celebrate God's life within the new baby. In telling her own early history she gives more detail about her Baptism than she does about her birth.

The lady in the kitchen

Frances was a lively, enterprising child who loved being out of doors and delighted in making friends. Lady Caroline Turnor, the young, newly wedded wife of the head of the local gentry family at Stoke Rochford Hall,

had been welcomed at the Hall by the Rector and his wife. The family, especially the girls, were looking forward to her return visit. Frances was out in the fields busy inspecting the flowers and insects, totally absorbed in the flourishing pond-life. She was unselfconsciously bespattered in mud when she heard a voice 'Hello, little girl, can you tell me how to get to the rectory?' 'Of course I can, I live there. I know a short-cut.' So the lady and a delighted, chattering Frances arrived at the back gate, through the vegetable garden and into the kitchen. The astounded family, caught without their parlour manners and formal propriety, gave their distinguished guest a spontaneously warm and affectionate welcome. For Lady Caroline, charmed by the natural friendliness of the young people, a happy contrast to a more conventional reception, this was the beginning of a life-long friendship.

This was just like Frances: devoid of affectation, secure in her knowledge of the love and fun in her family and ready to offer hospitality and to drop what she was doing to be of help to others. All these were traits of her developing personality and later characteristic of the founding spirit of the *Poor Servants of the Mother of God*, the religious congregation which she later founded. In later life when she had the formation of young religious as her main care, Frances disliked any affectation in the novices. A fussy, squeamish fear of spiders or moles or any wild life was firmly trained out

of the young women just as faddiness in food was not tolerated.

Another feature of her young life was her gift of telling stories. She would gather the little village children round her and tell them stories. When she had exhausted the patience of her own family she would sit telling stories to herself all the while weaving a piece of string in and out, round her fingers. The early sisters of The *Poor Servants of the Mother of God* would never disturb her when they saw her doing this, as they recognised the weaving to be an external part of her prayer, whilst she worked over her plans for the poor and for spreading God's reign.

In 1842 the happy family life was shattered by the death of their father on 19th June, from tuberculosis. His wife's diary reflects the heart-rending sorrow of a mother and her concern for her two youngest daughters, Lucy and Frances, who were to be sent to a boarding home for the daughters of impoverished clergymen. Lady Caroline intervened and offered to pay £50 per year for four years to avert this.

A teenager in London

On 13th August the broken-hearted family left Stoke Rochford to make their home in London in Cumberland Square, in a house loaned to the family until they found their own home. Frances recalled:

'There were few railways then and it was thought a great event to travel by rail. I had never been in a stage-coach even, so I began my life of travelling by railway.'

The family were soon living in Brompton and were happy to find nearby, in Holy Trinity Church, a very fervent parish with a lively congregation and a dedicated Vicar. They made many friends. One in particular, Maria O'Brien, later to become her sister-in-law, remembered her in this way:

'When I first knew her she was a bright, merry girl of twelve. The sisters were a happy band; they were not cast in the same mould, all were exemplary in their own way. I do not know of another such family and I am proud of belonging to them.'

Maria married the eldest son, George, in 1844. It was Maria who introduced the girls to the sights of London, taking them to museums and theatres. In good weather there were excursions to the Isle of Wight, Folkestone, Brighton and other resorts on the south coast.

Frances was not slow to notice London's two cities: one of wealth and privilege, the other of desperation and destitution. The historical city spoke to them from the very stones of past greatness and present wealth but also stared at them in the poverty and squalor of the lanes and 'rookeries' and in the hungry faces of the poor. Frances

took action and began to visit the sick poor in the workhouses accompanied by one of her sisters; her favourite outing in her home village had been going with her mother to the homes of the sick parishioners.

Following a family move to Regent's Park, two of the older Taylor girls, Emma and Charlotte, were deeply attracted to a nearby newly formed Anglican Sisterhood. Frances often joined the Sisters at Divine Office. When there was an outbreak of cholera in 1848, both Charlotte and Emma volunteered to go and help with Miss Priscilla Sellon's Anglican Sisterhood, which Emma then joined.

By 1853 Frances appears to have joined her two sisters to help with another outbreak of cholera in Devon. Charlotte confirmed in a letter that Frances was with her in Bristol where they were in charge of Miss Sellon's new hospital, a remarkable responsibility for two young women in their twenties. Charlotte and Frances eventually decided to return home, probably because they found the life and spirit of the Sisters too severe.

Crisis of faith

They both continued their fervent attendance in their local parish church, Christ Church, Albany Street. Here Rev. William Dodsworth held daily services and expounded Tractarian [High Church] doctrine, which held them spellbound. For Frances, the reverence of the curate Mr Gordon, especially when performing the rite of Baptism,

enthralled her. It clearly built on an early grace of insight into the reality of the sacrament, when the heart of the child became the dwelling place of God.

Now, every day brought news of eminent members of the Church of England changing their allegiance and becoming Catholic. Those who were priests usually went to Rome to be ordained as Catholic priests. There were many famous names among the people coming for guidance in the chaos that followed the so-called 'Gorham Judgement'. This was a controversy around the appointment to a parish by the Crown of a curate, Mr. Gorham who did not fully accept the theology of Baptism. His parochial appointment had already been blocked by his 'High Church' diocesan bishop.

Frances, in her late teens, would have been upset and confused. Her loyalty to the church of her parents and ancestors was unwavering but when people whom she admired, the priests who were most dedicated in her own parish, Rev. Dodsworth and later, Rev. Gordon, became Catholic, Frances was in turmoil herself. The anguish gone through by these men before making this decision was shared by very many thinking people.

The lady in the ragged school

Frances shared her perplexity with no one and went on with her daily visits to the workhouses and her teaching in the 'ragged' school for street boys. The boys were

enticed off the streets with the promise of bread and treacle. She was alone in a makeshift classroom with fifty boys, many of them anxious to learn to read and write but some were there for fun. Frances was very tall and was said to look older than her years, but faced with a roomful of tough boys who used their physical strength to terrify the neighbourhood, she confessed to feeling 'mortal terror in her heart'. If they misbehaved Frances had no sanction except to order the culprits to leave but one day a big, tough lad refused to budge and the rest of the group sat grinning. She knew her only chance was to remain outwardly calm, if she failed now she would lose her authority for ever. She appealed to the gallantry of the biggest lad there who stood up and said. 'Lookee, here, mates I'm a-going to stand by this 'ere lady. And if you don't go Bill, I'll make you!' The whole room sided with him and Bill went. The 'school' became a success and the lives of many of the boys were changed for the better.

Crimean Nursing

The Crimean War broke out in 1854 and, too soon, England was shocked by the reports of injured soldiers dying from lack of medical care. The great need was for nurses. Frances did not volunteer with the first group of ladies to travel with Florence Nightingale. Her uncharacteristic delay in acting would appear to point to the inner struggle and the search for God's will; her spiritual director urged her to volunteer, but she stayed at home.

Journey to war

However, by 1st December 1854 she was one of forty-seven women to travel to the front. There were fifteen Sisters of Mercy from England and Ireland; there were lady volunteers and there were 'paid nurses' who had experience of working in hospitals in England's main cities. A number of the latter had come in the hope of nursing their husbands but many of them had to be sent home because of their drunken behaviour. Nursing was not yet considered a profession. Hospital work was dangerous and conditions were filthy and infectious. Normally, it was retired prostitutes, pickpockets and worn-out charwomen who were the 'paid nurses'.

The journey to Constantinople took nineteen terrifying days. The vessel was a 'rickety, un-seaworthy boat', retrieved from demolition to serve as a troop-ship. They cast anchor at Messina for repairs and the ladies took advantage of the stop and went to see the sights. The Sisters felt they should stay on board. Frances, though delighted with the fresh air and the freedom to see the lovely town, thought of those who had to stay on board. The diaries of the Mercy nuns tell us: 'Our dearest friend Miss Taylor, refreshed us by her gift of beautiful orange blossoms which filled our berth with fragrance.'

Following more storms and further repairs to the ship at Navarino, on 17th December they were within sight of Constantinople. Frances wrote:

'No travellers had ever before had their attention distracted from the beautiful panorama of Constantinople, we had eyes only for the hospitals, goal of our long journey ... How our hearts longed to be in those hospitals, to be soothing in some small degree a portion of the mighty mass of suffering.'

Mary Stanley, who was leader of this group, disembarked to meet Florence Nightingale, later returning to say there was 'no room for them' in Scutari. The idea of sending them straight home appeared so monstrous at a moment when fifteen hundred sick men were arriving from Balaclava that the Ambassador resolved to do all in his power to utilise their services.

Unwelcome nurses

Frances later wrote:

'We could not find out why we were detained and whose fault it was. Wherever the fault lay it was most unaccountable that 47 women should be kept idle ... while the hospitals were crowded. The deaths at Scutari had risen from 165 in September to 667 in December and to 90 per day amounting to 1473 in January. There were at this time only 10 nurses at the General Hospital. Houses were easily acquired for other purposes so why should we not be accommodated? If we had been allowed to help in the cooking, there were but 12 cooks for upward of 3,000 sick, it would have alleviated much of the suffering of the poor patients.'

According to France's account, whilst the prospective nurses waited, two of them visited the naval hospital, spoke to the men and wrote letters for them; we may reasonably suppose that Frances was one of these two.

It was 15th January before fifteen of the waiting women were called to Scutari. Frances describes:

'The hospital was crowded to its fullest extent; the building, reckoned to hold, with comfort, seventeen hundred men, held nearly three thousand. The number of patients under my care with one nurse and another lady was about one thousand.

'As we passed the corridors, we asked ourselves if this were not a terrible dream. When we woke in the morning, our hearts sank at the thought of the woe we must witness during the day. At night we lay down wearied beyond expression; but not so much from physical fatigue, though that was great, as from sickness of heart occasioned by living amidst such a mass of hopeless suffering.'

Frustrated carers

Red-tape strangled the good services of the nurses. Drinks or nourishment of any kind could not be given to a patient without a written requisition by the doctor. Even when allowed, the water was lethal until Frances took the initiative to boil water and make beef-tea or lemonade.

These drinks were bliss to the parched patients until an order from the Inspector General stopped all 'cooking' in the wards.

Frances writes (*emphasis mine*):

'It was very sad work … to pace the corridors and hear the low voice of a fever patient "Give me a drink for the love of God!" and have none to give … or to see the look of disappointment on the faces of those to whom we had been accustomed to give beef tea. The assistant surgeons were very sorry; but they had no power to help it – their duty was only to obey … Amid

all the confusion and distress of Scutari hospital, *military discipline was never lost sight of, and an infringement of one of its smallest observances was worse than letting twenty men die from neglect.'*

Frances often took charge or claimed responsibility for acting in a crisis. She may have been the youngest nurse but she was quick to take action in preventing soldiers newly arrived from the battlefield from being placed in wards or beds contaminated by fever. Scutari Hospital had been built on open sewers, small wonder 14,000 died in the wards.

Frances was one of the first to volunteer to go to Koulali Hospital. The number of patients there was very high but the site was more hygienic and the greatest relief was to hear the doctors say: 'Give the men whatever they want.'

On 1st February ship-loads of wounded arrived, and the orderlies had to put up beds, for there were none vacant. All the nurses that could be spared from the wards went to get food ready for the newcomers. There was no kitchen range so wood fires were lighted and cauldrons of hot water prepared. Some nurses fed the exhausted men, others washed their hands and faces, cut off their long, matted hair and replaced their vermin-ridden clothes with clean shirts. Many men with frost-bitten limbs had to face surgery, carried out in the wards. There were no anaesthetics for any surgery, least of all for amputations

and many did not survive. It took six orderlies to hold down the patient and others had to stuff their ears to drown the screams.

Nightly intruders

In Koulali the atmosphere was less bigoted and the patients were the main focus of care. There was no discrimination in allocating supplies or in using everything from the 'gift store' sent generously from England. Bad management and red-tape had meant that much needed supplies were left to be eaten by rats or rot in the harbour. Frances and all the lady volunteers suffered from a plague of rats in their house at Koulali Hospital:

'They galloped about the ceiling like a squadron of horses. At night they walked about our bedrooms, jumped upon our pillows, licked or chewed at our hair, they would jump from stair to stair sounding like a man's heavy footstep. Often did we rise, thinking there must be people moving about, only to find it was our usual visitors.'

The rat experience ruined her sleep; she was to suffer from insomnia for the rest of her life.

The lady at the well

Any incident that might redound to her own credit Frances usually wrote in the third person. Luckily we have the version of the Sisters of Mercy:

'When the dreadful times of sickness and death came and many things were wanting for the sick soldiers, Miss Taylor would go at 3 a.m. to get supplies from the French Hospital. When fresh water failed she would go all the long distance to the well, with pitchers for the precious water, before it was polluted by the herdsmen and their animals. She carried the water back where it was most needed.'

Soldiers on the battlefield were lucky to hold on to their lives. When injured, their knapsacks and contents were often the first things to be lost. Requests for replacements often faced the intransigence and bureaucracy of the military purveyor's department. Frances applied to the very humane Commissioner Stow, who had charge of *The Times Fund*. She handed him a list and everything on it was supplied the following day.

Frances described her feelings:

'My heart was too sad and weary at the hourly deaths of young men cut down in the flower of youth to enter any controversy about the Authorities and Commissioner Stow. I only knew this: one let the men die for the want of things, the other provided them. His last act was to give leave to buy all the available fruit in season for the soldiers. He died shortly afterwards but will be forever remembered for his courtesy, his kind and friendly manner with which he cheered the sinking hearts that had struggled through this time of misfortune.'

Frances was very touched by the faith of the Irish soldiers. She found that they spoke of Jesus and Mary as though they were members of their own family and of dying as 'going home'. She would always send for the Catholic Chaplain to attend to their last rites but she was a bit shaken by the English soldiers of the same rank whose vague hope when they were nearing their end was 'that God wouldn't be too hard on them'.

Miss Smythe, one of the ladies who had come to Koulali, contracted the virulent fever which had taken many soldiers recovering from their wounds. Frances tells us she was serving the men's dinners when word came Miss Smythe had died. 'Such was our life at the time that I had to go on serving the dinners before I could go to the death-bed.'

Letter-writer

Frances always had time to be with the men in the loneliness of their last hours. She wrote of one man, very seriously wounded, whose age was guessed to be fifty. He recovered slightly and was able to tell them his date of birth, he was nineteen. He couldn't bear to give anybody trouble and one night Frances stayed up with him as his usual nurse had contracted fever. The man wept at the idea of keeping Frances from her night's sleep. Practical as ever she said: 'I am a strong woman, perfectly well able to stay with you. When the day nurse comes I shall

go to bed myself. There is no point in your making yourself more ill with weeping, when you need sleep.' She discovered he had lost his whole family to the famine and the poorhouse convinced him he was of no value. So he wept because 'the lady' cared enough to give up her night's sleep to look after him.

One great need was to have letters written home for the men either because of illness or inability to write. There was nowhere for the letter-writer to sit or kneel except on the floor. Frances tells us she wept so much as she wrote the letters that she had to rewrite them because her tears too often blotted the page. However, her sense of humour helped to relieve the horror. She writes:

'I would begin with: "What shall I say?"

"Just anything you like, Miss, just the same as you write in your own letters home."

"But how shall I begin?" "Dear Thomas"

I write on then, hoping dear Thomas is well and informing him of the illness and whereabouts of his friend. Then I ask: "Is Thomas a relation?"

"Oh! He's just my father, Miss"

"But shouldn't I address him properly?"

"Oh, never mind Miss; it's all the same – it will do very well." '

Frances had the gift of bringing out talents in the soldiers. Those recovering or waiting for transport home, had time on their hands. Frances soon had them making presents for the other soldiers and nurses; some discovered a gift for sketching, indeed the illustrations in her book *Eastern Hospitals and English Nurses* were made by one of the soldiers. One man wrote poetry and his ballads were hilarious but she adds: 'I regret I cannot share them with my readers!'

A New Catholic

Frances had protested to the authorities about the injustice of allowing the men to suffer, especially when remedies were available in the stores. She was called a proselytiser because she made no secret of her unease at the treatment given by authorities to the Mercy Sisters. Her candid protests did not endear her to the powers in charge. Her whole experience of faith, as she saw it practised, brought her misgivings to a head. She wrote: 'I was alone, the lady companions had all gone, one had died, the others were invalided home. I was anxiously expecting another party from England to help me. I was very High Church and devoted to the nuns.'

I met the Good Shepherd

On Easter Monday, April 1855 her sister Charlotte arrived among a group of volunteers. They were a joyful bunch still full of the fun and laughter they had on the journey. The main cause of hilarity had been Father Sidney Woollett SJ. Charlotte spoke highly of his help on the journey and Frances was very concerned that Charlotte seemed too impressed by Catholic thinking. So Frances made an appointment to see him, presumably to ask him not to influence Charlotte.

During the week that Fr Woollett was at Koulali, we do not know how he probed her reasons for being so concerned about Charlotte's faith. What we do know is that Frances stayed on to acknowledge her own doubts. Fr Woollett had himself become a Catholic following the death of his beloved wife. Far from rescuing Charlotte from being 'Romanised', Frances returned every day for discussions on points of faith that were confusing to her. Life at that time was very precarious; the deaths of two Sisters of Mercy and of Miss Smythe had had a profound effect on Frances and she struggled continuously between her need to be loyal, her need to be at peace with her own conscience, and her wish to follow where God seemed to be leading. She was received into the Church on 14th April and made her First Communion on Good Shepherd Sunday, at the hands of Fr William Ronan SJ. Fr Woollett was not present, for he had already gone to take up his duties at the battle front. Frances was deeply happy when she was told she had no need of a second baptism. However, she had to keep her conversion secret for fear of the authorities.

'Father Woollett SJ came back several months later to recuperate from fever. I remember how he used to teach me, walking by the Bosphorus in the moonlight and in those odd days that did not seem odd, some of his instructions on prayer, vocation, the love of God, shown by preference not by feelings, I never forgot. In

religious life, he said, you become part of a body, no self allowed, and whatever we did the spirit of prayer was to be everything. We lived under the reign of terror but Fr Woollett said we should take the bull by the horns. So we had Mass said in any spot where a priest could be safely found. The instructions along the Bosphorus, confession in a corner of the ward kitchen: it was fine preparation for a convert.'

The Church of the Second Spring

All the lady volunteers returned to England on 22nd November 1855. The chief medical officer wrote to Mary Stanley, the leader of the group Frances had arrived with:

'It was ungrateful to permit you and Miss Taylor to quit the hospital, and not express my profound sense of the exalted influence for good your presence and the services you have conferred upon this establishment have had. I have daily witnessed your and their unwearied, intelligent and truly feminine ministrations in aiding my professional labours ... hence this dutiful expression of my sentiments with the wish to bid you goodbye in the spirit of thankfulness and respect.'

On 14th December they were called on deck to see the shores of England. Frances now faced the pain of telling her mother she had become a Catholic. There is no record of how the news was received but there are entries in the

mother's diaries which indicate the huge breach in relations with her youngest and, it seems, most loved child.

A Victorian's comment

Frances had to begin writing immediately in response to Mary Stanley's strong request 'to make the truth known about our war': *Eastern Hospitals and English Nurses* was published in 1856. It was certainly one of the first published accounts of the Crimean War to appear. This tribute appeared in *Colburn's United Services Magazine and Naval Military Journal* in May of that year, addressed 'To the unknown author, Volunteer Nurse' (*emphasis mine*):

'One of the charms of this book is its unconscious reflection of the character of its author. We see her gentle spirit flitting through every page, as she did through the wards of Scutari and Koulali – softly, silently, always with the same kind, endearing look, the same tender sympathy: not rigid and sombre, but fresh and blooming, with a smile on her lip and now and then, a joke too, yes actually a joke, but so innocent and harmless, that a saint might hear it! *She tells us what every one did but herself*, how they exerted themselves, what they suffered, how nobly they behaved – Protestants, Catholics, Dissenters, it matters not; for these holy women whatever their

sect, were all Christians. They had that most excellent gift of charity, which devises no ill, and they loved each other as they loved their kind. There is a sweet cheerfulness, at times even vivacity, in this good lady's narrative, bursting upon us unawares, yet ever blended with a flow of feeling which nothing can intercept. At the right moment she raises our eyes from the bed of death to the life beyond, and shows how it is possible to be devout without being gloomy. In a word, her book gives us a better impression of our nature, inspiring a more charitable disposition towards our fellow-creatures, and a more thankful heart to God.'

Eastern Hospitals and English Nurses appeared in its third edition in 1857. It was a best-seller. The final chapter in the book is a plea for professional training and status for nursing. The third edition adds a tribute to the Sisters of Mercy in the penultimate chapter. The entire book is a reflection of Frances' mind and hopes. The final paragraph to the first two editions reads:

'Nursing is a work that can be done rightly by those who can offer body and soul as a daily sacrifice, and in that offering find their joy and consolation, whose sole desire is to follow in the steps of Jesus who came 'not to be served but to serve'.'

Inspiration

The 1857 Edition of *Eastern Hospitals* adds:

'Oh! That someone would rise up with burning eloquence enough to plead the cause of English poor… and awaken in us all a spirit of union and charity, that we may join in the great work of succouring the poor, not by doling out to them alms of this world's goods, but by those words and acts which can make them feel we have alike one hope, one end, one Master.'

This, and her deep appreciation of the mystery of God living within each human person, is the key that unlocks the call and the founding grace of *The Poor Servants of the Mother of God*. It gives words to the spirit of Frances Taylor, it puts the Incarnation at the heart of our lives and the way in which we become the presence of God in the world. Believing in this, the only way Frances could spend the rest of her life was in revealing this insight through deep reverence for every person.

The years from the age of twenty-four to thirty-seven are adulthood, life establishing itself. For Frances Taylor they were a time of being alive, of searching for what that life meant to her and what it was to be for others. She had joined a Church reaping the fruits of Catholic Emancipation. She wanted to serve the poor and the suffering. London in 1856 was the richest capital city in the world, centre of a great colonial empire, it was the

fastest growing capital. The sad fact was that its wealth was matched only by the depths of its poverty.

Frances returned there, aged twenty-three, precipitated into adulthood by the spiritual and personal experiences of her time in the Crimea. She went straight into writing her *Eastern Hospitals and English Nurses*. Throughout her life she had an extraordinary power of concentration; whatever task she had on hand she could give it her total attention. This meant she always had time to live. Her sister-in-law, Maria O'Brien who had described 'the bright, merry girl of twelve', now saw 'she had become a helpful, kind and loving woman; one whom no one who knew her could help loving.'

She was soon the centre of a group of lively young women, among them her sisters Charlotte and Lucy, Maria O'Brien, a Mary Gunning and, perhaps, a Lydia Bennett whom she had first known in Miss Sellon's Sisterhood. By August 1857 Charlotte too had become a Catholic. Mary Gunning, (who eventually became a Daughter of Charity of St Vincent de Paul) later wrote about their daily lives:

'The two sisters rose early and attended Mass daily. The morning hours were devoted to writing; in the afternoon hospitals and poor people in the workhouses of St Pancras were visited. I never saw Frances without real work in hand … It was at this time *Tyborne* was

written. I remember with what pleasure I listened to the manuscript, the chapters of the day's work being read in the evening, and how it consoled the dear writer to see my tears flow as the beautiful passages came forth … I loved her more than any person I ever knew.'

Frances had gone to Dr Henry Manning, Parish Priest of St Mary of the Angels, Bayswater, to ask for Spiritual Direction, which he generously gave. He put her in the way of helping unemployed or poor working girls, London's maidservants, factory workers and seamstresses. For the Sundays in Lent of 1859 she needed another larger room since the first brave souls to come brought their friends. They had a schoolroom at Bayswater where they met for prayer and preparation for the Sacraments. Afterwards they had tea, bread and treacle, prepared by Frances who would join in the repast herself and they would have stories and laughter as well as teaching of scripture stories, then all of them would go to St Mary of the Angels for Evening Prayer.

Popular author

Frances helped to fill the gap left by centuries of prohibition against Catholic publications by writing articles, historical novels and very popular serial stories, all with a Christian Catholic content.

In her twenties Frances was to use her gift for story-telling to rescue her family from financial difficulties. Dr Manning encouraged her writing and the money it made also helped her work for the poor. She was soon to need to be financially independent. Her brother George, who was the head of the family, made some unwise investments, and Frances was forced to take over the management of the family finances, and support her mother.

Searching for God's will

All the time Frances ardently wished to give her life completely to God, but how? She had accompanied Mary Gunning to Paris in 1859 when Mary was entering the Daughters of Charity. Frances herself felt attracted to the life of a Sister of Charity. She arranged to come back in January 1861 to try her vocation by a prolonged visit to the Novitiate house. She was there two weeks. Everything Frances was attracted to seemed to be there. She loved the Sisters and they loved her. But instead of peace, she experienced a storm of inner fear and unease. Her great wish was to find and do God's will but Père Etienne, the Superior-General, was sure her call was not for the Daughters of Charity. He had a great regard for Frances but felt her gift for writing books helpful to English readers would be lost in Paris.

Frances returned still struggling in a dark sea of uncertainty. Her reflection on the experiences was:

'I don't think it was right for me to leave home. Home cares were a burden to me; I wanted to get rid of them and go and be, as I thought, happy in a convent. I think God permitted me to go because the Lord knew nothing else would teach me such a lesson.'

Meanwhile, her sister Charlotte had married Edward Dean, also a convert. Frances became editor of *The Lamp* from 1862 to 1871. In 1864 she was asked by the Jesuit fathers to be responsible for editing *The Month*, which was a magazine for readers of serious social and church issues. Frances found it to be very onerous and was relieved to hand it back to the Jesuits at the end of the year. Before that, however, she had applied to John Henry Newman in desperation for contributions. The story goes he was too busy to write anything just then, but he offered her his meditational poem on the blissful passing of the soul into *the presence of God: it was called The Dream of Gerontius*. First published in *The Month* it was made even more famous by Elgar's musical setting.

A name which continually appeared on the pages of *The Month* was that of Lady Georgiana Fullerton. A saintly, gracious benefactor of many good causes, she became a true friend to Frances. They got on well: Frances was an ardent admirer of Lady Georgiana's writing and she found a wise head and unselfish heart when she needed to discuss her own future.

The next attempt to enter religious life came from discovering the Filles de Marie, known in England as the Daughters of the Heart of Mary. These Sisters, founded during the French Revolution, had never worn a religious habit nor did they live together in a convent. They lived with their families, had a rule and took vows.

Frances wrote:

'I feel this strong attraction and it will end all doubts and perplexities about my family. If I am told to stay it will be obedience for me and if it is not I shall come away.'

It was not for her. The reason given was that her character was too formed and she would find obedience too hard.

Frances discussed the outcome with Lady Georgiana and they decided to pray and wait for God's will to become clear. Lady Georgiana went to Italy and while there prayed for guidance. She had a vivid inspiration about the kind of religious life in which Frances would thrive: a group of women living together in faith, sharing prayer and supporting each other's faith, hope and love and going out to their daily work. At that very time Frances had the same experience in prayer. She felt very much at peace and both friends believed this was God's plan.

Frances knew her deepest call was to work for the poor in cities. In London the people who were 'poorer than the poor' were the immigrants from Ireland. They, who had

inspired such respect in her through their unselfish heroism, good-humour and generosity whilst recovering from war wounds, were like a different race in England. Destitution had corrupted them and driven them to crime.

If she were to help the Irish, her friend thought she should see the Irish in their home setting, in order to understand their homes and upbringing. The plan was that Frances should visit Ireland and see what was being done there for the poor. There was a hidden agenda, never expressed, but it looked as though Frances hoped she would be able to attract some aspirants to come and undertake the work she saw needed to be done in London.

Her experiences were to be written up and sent as articles for publication in *The Lamp*. The articles were so popular that they were revised and collected into one volume in 1867 called *Irish Homes and Irish Hearts*. The dedication reads:

> 'To Those Who, under strange skies and amid the still stranger scenes of Eastern Hospitals, first taught me the Worth of Irish Character, the warmth of Irish Hearts, and the depths of Irish Faith, this little book is dedicated.'

One review said: 'This book might serve as a text-book on the Irish question'. Frances herself wrote in the first chapter, referring to the historic legacy of injustice inflicted by the English State on the Catholic Irish: 'I

believe that the evil of England's misunderstanding of Ireland would be obviated if English people would remember what Irish people would do well to forget.'

The book is a classic of travel, and study of Irish religious and social history. It is a charming book to read and, although the information may be out of date, it gives a marvellous insight into post-famine Ireland; but also it tells us a great deal about Frances herself. Her humour; her burning anger against the injustice of punishing a people for remaining loyal to their faith; her ability to enjoy life: all of these make it still an engrossing read.

The reluctant founder

Frances returned from her visits to Ireland full of admiration for all the good being done by religious for the poor. She convinced Dr Manning and Lady Georgiana that nothing then existing seemed to fulfil the ideal God had placed before them. She knew not yet how it was to be brought about. It was still a vague unformed vision.

For her, the poor were the social companions of Jesus and Mary, not merely unfortunate or unemployed people. Her great wish was to work with them as well as for them. She had misgivings about the class system as it was mirrored in the convents: women with dowries became Choir Nuns often with the title 'Mother' the others became Lay Sisters. Frances did not articulate this but when she did found her own Congregation there were to

be no differences in rank and the lack of a dowry was never to be an obstacle to joining a community.

Two women, Mary Ward, and an unnamed older aspirant whom Frances 'thought would be capable of carrying on the work', moved into four small rooms in a little court leading out of Fleet Street on 24th October 1868. Frances Taylor joined them every day to pray and work with them and Lady Georgiana brought a statue of Our Lady (still preserved in the heritage centre in St Mary's Convent, Brentford, Middlesex). They placed the new religious family under Our Lady's protection. A month passed and troubles arose. The neighbours objected to the poor people coming to the house and the Sisters prayed for guidance. Before they had to leave, Frances was in touch with the mission in Tower Hill run by the Oblate Fathers and the community moved there on 23rd January, 1869.

Unfortunately, the health of the older postulant, who had shown such promise, shortly broke down completely and she had to go home, and Mary Ward also left shortly after. However, two young women, Frances McCarthy and Bathia Deverill, a widow, expressed an interest in working with Frances. On 2nd February they took possession of a small house in Chamber Street, Tower Hill; once again Our Lady was installed as the Superior. They were in great poverty; there was scarcely any furniture in the house. Towards the end of the month Frances came to live with the community; her beloved

mother's death had left Frances heart-broken but free of all home responsibilities. She did not refer to this great loss in her diary. It was a grief too deep for words.

The daily life in Chamber Street was all work: an industrial school by day and night classes for enthusiastic groups. The demands of the large poor population left them with little time to do anything about living a balanced life of prayer and work. The little community worked in this very poor mission for a period of approximately eighteen months, until another congregation took over the work.

Lady Georgiana had met a priest, Fr Biemans, who told them about Sisters in Poland, Little Servants of the Mother of God, who lived in community and worked directly with poor peasant families. In August Frances set out to investigate. Her trip took three weeks and was a whirlwind tour of Austrian, German, and Polish territory, terrifying in some ways, amusing in others but overall enlightening. Frances met the Founder, (now) St Edmund Bojanowski, who made a lasting, profound impression on her.

She wrote to Lady Georgiana, referring to Father James Clare SJ, who had by this time become Frances's spiritual director (*emphasis mine*):

'I am sure Father Clare SJ was right to send me, nothing else would have done. It was necessary for well founding our work, but you must pray. *The more I*

see of foreign orders the more convinced I am we must found our own. They have done it and so must we. The nuns who are so anxious to go to England have no idea of the difficulties. Then I think in dismay 'Am I fit to undertake such a work?' and I wonder what you and Fr Clare can be thinking about. The founders of these congregations are probably very holy people. *My only hope is that if I make a beginning, God will raise up someone to continue the work.'*

So at last the puzzle is solved. Thirteen years had passed since she talked about religious life with Fr Woollett SJ on the shores of the Bosphorus. She had struggled to find God's will. Could it be that part of the struggle was her fear of responsibility? Yet Frances had always taken responsibility as the easiest thing in the world. Perhaps her innate humility was the main reason why she had avoided even letting herself question if God could possibly choose her, a convert, to be a founder. On her return from Poland Fr Clare SJ suggested that Frances make a discernment retreat. Her 'Polish' journey was a critical experience for her in the following of Jesus Christ. Her spirituality had been formed from childhood: her graphic insight into the indwelling of the Trinity; a profound, personal friendship with the Lord; such experiences had to become the subject of deep reflection before she could accept the road she was being called to

follow. She made a discernment list with reasons for and against making a new beginning. She once again veered toward an already established order.

Entering a contemplative order was high on the list but did not survive Fr Clare's scrutiny. The Polish idea seemed to offer a way of beginning. Nowhere on the list does the thought occur that she herself should found a new Congregation. Father Clare had no problem in sifting out what was influenced by fear and what was a form of escapism. The attraction to a fully contemplative life was exactly that, a way out for her. He knew the union of contemplation and action was right for Frances. He saw, too, the Lord had long ago called her to work with the poor in great cities. Dr Manning, who was now Archbishop of Westminster, had continued his interest and support of Frances in her spiritual search, and he heartily agreed with Fr Clare.

Small beginnings

The result of the retreat was so immediate that on 24th September 1869 Father James Clare SJ, authorised by Archbishop Manning, received as postulants: Frances Taylor, Frances McCarthy and Bathia Deverill. Their names in religion were:

Frances Taylor: Mary Magdalen
Frances McCarthy: Mary Colette
Bathia Deverill: Mary Elizabeth

On 12th February 1872 Frances Taylor took her Final Vows, and this date is now kept by *The Poor Servants of the Mother of God* as their founding day. The 'Polish idea' excellent in rural settings, became impractical for city conditions but nevertheless the Poor Servants retained an affectionate relationship with the Sisters in a divided Poland, empathising with their sufferings amid the disruptions of many wars.

Frances was placed in charge of the group of Postulants and she asked that Lady Georgiana give instructions to them. Lady Georgiana consulted the Jesuit Fathers about the request and the saintly lady was told she should 'do nothing of the kind. Mother Magdalen is the right person; she is quite capable of giving instructions herself.'

The community had from October 1869 rented a cottage in Robert Street near to Grosvenor Square, in central London, later moving permanently to a larger property not far away at the rear of Cavendish Square. At first they tried to support themselves by needlework and the manufacture of military coats, but this was found not to be sustainable.

Frances wrote of these early days:

'We were very poor, but very happy. We had great spiritual blessings being so near Farm Street where Father Clare was Rector. Hardly anyone knew we were

religious, we passed as poor working women, unknown and unnoticed.'

But they were noticed and somebody in Farm Street congregation called them 'Poor Clares.' What began as a joke cost Father Clare some embarrassment when there was an enquiry set afoot by the diocese!

Frances writes:

'By Easter we had made up our minds that we could not support the community by needlework. Catherine Burrows, a postulant, understood laundry work and though we had no idea how to begin we prayed to Our Lady to help us. The idea of laundry work was accepted, at any rate as a means of supporting the community. We began on 1st May. It was humble work; it was the closest imitation of the work of the Holy Family of Nazareth.'

From friends came ridicule and opposition but Frances thought, 'Wasn't Jesus known as the son of a carpenter?' However, no laundry work came so they prayed twice as hard. Frances got the inspiration to visit a wealthy lady and tell her what they wanted. 'From that moment she took up our work then others sent theirs; by 31st May we had more than we could do and were compelled to look for a new house.'

Frances also writes: 'During the month of June we suffered from excessive heat and from over-work; we

could not refuse washing, but had to get through it as best we could.'

The cottage in Robert Street was very small, so they prayed and rather miraculously were offered the house in Cavendish Square to rent, the front of which was used as a studio. They entered by a side lane but the rooms were airy and spacious, a God-given answer to prayer. Perhaps because Frances had such experience in being homeless and in searching for suitable houses, her friends to this day invoke her aid when they know of people trying to buy or to sell a house.

Joys and sorrows

Their first visitor in Cavendish Square was Father Edward Healy O.M.I. It had been his wisdom which dictated the removal from Tower Hill since he could see the young religious congregation needed time for formation in prayer. He was very pleased with the house and promised to say the first Mass there. He was on his way to Inchicore in Dublin to make his annual retreat and he arranged to meet Frances afterwards. He had two postulants to recommend to her and she found strength in his wisdom and sound advice for the future. He promised he would give the novices instructions throughout the winter.

Frances left him on 12th September as he hoped to catch the mail-boat the following morning. She herself went to Wexford on 14th September, in order to visit the

Marie Reparatrice (later Perpetual Adoration) convent there; as she was leaving Dublin heard the newsboys cry: 'Fatal accident to night mail, lives lost'. She bought a paper, and to her horror saw one priest had been killed on the railway between Holyhead and London. She travelled to Wexford in extreme anxiety, hoping against hope he had travelled in the morning as he had planned. When she reached Wexford her fears were confirmed. Father Healy had indeed been killed. Aged thirty-one, his death was an enormous loss to his own congregation and, for Frances, a deep personal sorrow.

Poor Servant of the Mother of God

The convent in Wexford had been founded, in 1868 at the request of Bishop Furlong, by Mother Joseph (Lydia Bennett), an associate of the Founder of the Congregation of Marie Reparatrice, Blessed Amelie D'Hooghvorst. In September 1870 Mother Joseph was struggling with money worries and all the concerns of a new foundation. She had been a friend of Frances since they were both in their teens. This is her account of this visit from Frances:

Show me your friends

'Frances felt she had lost her best earthly friend; she was depending on him to help her in the establishing of her new Institute. Yet, having poured out her soul in the Chapel she put herself at my disposal, knowing I was experiencing a time of great difficulty.'

Frances thought she could best help Mother Joseph by introducing her to some friends in Dublin who had promised financial help to Frances. They set out together for Enniscorthy in an outside car but the convents there had been warned that there were criminals on the move, preying on people for money and dressed as 'strange

nuns.' Frances and Joseph received a very cold welcome even from the curate.

Frances was astounded, 'Could they not see we were ladies!'

'Well,' [continues Mother Joseph Bennett], 'we were dressed in shabby black, as far as I can remember, and not in any way to inspire confidence. But Frances was so perfectly unconscious of her appearance; she never even gave a thought of how she looked. When her life is written, I think this complete unselfconsciousness should be brought out in bold relief, for it was most remarkable in her. I think this was one of her most remarkable qualities … We were at last given a cup of tea but Frances was not satisfied for me to go without a dinner, so she discovered a shop, a kind of eating house. She put me into the waiting room at the railway station and very soon she arrived back carrying a picnic basket with ham and chicken, bread and claret, glasses, knives and forks.'

In Dublin the money that had been promised for the young community in Cavendish Square was diverted to help the struggling group in Wexford.

Frances said not a word of this. All she mentions is:

'The friendship and encouragement and great kindness I received from the nuns in Wexford, who though in great difficulty with their new foundation, took a warm interest in ours.'

When holy people begin telling stories of each other it is difficult to know what standards to apply. What we are sure of is both founders remained friends, supportive of each other's undertakings in prayer and practical means for as long as they lived.

Frances had a gift for friendships. Those she made during the Crimean war were kept fresh. Their convents were her stopping places during her tour of Ireland recorded in *Irish Homes and Irish Hearts*.

Mother Francis Bridgeman was the Superior of the Mercy convent in Kinsale, Ireland, and had been leader of the contingent of Sisters of Mercy at Koulali Hospital. She had given lessons in nursing care to all who were interested. Frances always included Kinsale in her visits to Ireland and she received advice and, later on, she also received postulants who were interested in the mission to the Irish poor in England. Mother Bridgeman appreciated the ready humour of Frances and the sisters loved to see the two friends sharing memories and providing many an evening of laughter and stories from the Crimean war. One such evening the two friends were seated on a window seat enjoying the lovely view of old Kinsale Harbour when Mother Magdalen moved her hand and, not seeing a crack in the window pane, accidently smashed it outright. 'Ah!' said Mother Bridgeman, 'that's an English fist!' Her friend turned, holding up a bleeding fist, 'And that's Irish glass, see, it has paid me off.'

Frances Taylor had established a community in Carrigtwohill, County Cork, in 1875, which is still there to this day. During a visit by Frances to the convent in Carrigtwohill in 1883, the community were in retreat and the Founder herself took care of answering the door. When the bell rang she found a tall man, on his way home from Mass, asking for his copy of *The Sacred Heart Messenger*. As he reached out to take it she noticed one hand was badly injured with several fingers missing. She kindly took the hand in hers and said, 'Dear me, poor man, that looks like a war wound?' He said, 'I almost lost that hand at the Crimean War. I know that voice; were you ever at Koulali yourself?' Frances said she had been there but was not a Sister then, and the man became overcome, weeping aloud. He was brought in and they shared a cup of tea together. He told his wife and family that he had met the 'noblest and kindest person in the world when he was sure she was dead from the hardships of that dreadful place. She saved our lives and kept us sane out there.' He spoke of working on the London docks after the war until Dr. Manning heard his mother was ill and alone in Cork and organised a transfer for him to Hawlbowline. Every time Frances went to Carrigtwohilll Mr Coffey visited her and took her to visit his own home.

Frances' priests

Naturally Frances formed deep friendships with the priests who directed her throughout her life. Father Woollett SJ, who witnessed her reception into the Catholic Church, she stayed in touch with, and went to visit him in Stonyhurst when he retired there in 1893. Father Dignam SJ shared his passionate devotion to the Sacred Heart of Jesus with Frances, who helped to him in promoting the Apostleship of Prayer. This was a society set up to enable a daily offering of the member's whole day, joys and sorrows, through the Sacred Heart of Jesus to the Father. On one visit to Dublin Frances was asked by Fr Dignam to see if she could do anything to revive the Sacred Heart Devotion in Ireland.

Fr James Cullen SJ had been known to her in Wexford as a friend of Mother Joseph Bennett's, when he was a one of Bishop Furlong's Missioners. Frances met him in a Dublin bookshop and asked him what he was doing for the Apostleship of Prayer. He made a lame excuse and Frances said, 'You are worse since you became a Jesuit' (this was a saintly man famous for the extraordinary retreats). He replied, 'I don't require you to tell me that; my *Particular Examen* (examination of conscience) tells me every day.' 'Well,' she replied 'put your *Particular Examen* on your neglect of the Apostleship'.

Frances's goading was apparently to bear fruit, for only shortly afterwards Fr Cullen became Central Director of the Apostleship in Ireland, and in 1888 he established the *Irish Messenger of the Sacred Heart*. In six month's time the *Irish Messenger* was publishing tens of thousands of copies and the Apostleship of Prayer was established all over the country. It was the monthly reading material of many a home that could not afford a newspaper. The poet, Patrick Kavanagh, said he depended on this monthly spiritual sustenance and read it from cover-to-cover.

Father Augustus Dignam SJ had been attracted to the spirit and spirituality of Frances so well embodied in The Poor Servants of the Mother of God. He was to be her guide and mentor from their first meeting in 1873 until the end of his life. He was much loved by the early Sisters. Frances collected his instructions, all his retreats and conferences and had them published. They sold in Europe but also in Australia and America.

She was compiler and editor. In an age where handwritten manuscripts were not the usual route to the publisher one marvels at her energy and industry in spreading religious reading through her great number of publications. She was not encouraged in this when it came to writing the *Life of Father Dignam SJ*.

A fellow Jesuit, Father Cooksey wrote this about Frances:

'As you know the idea of a life of any of ours being published at all, or at any rate soon after their death is out of the question, 'it is just not done'. One day before I left Manresa, Father Purbrick, the Provincial, came into the Juniors' room with a letter in his hand. He told us Mother Frances Taylor had already written a Life of Father Dignam and she had sent it to him for his approval! I think she had also asked him to write the Preface. He had written her a long letter, in the hope of suppressing that attempt at once, criticising the whole thing without mercy: "And now, look here. This is a letter from her THANKING me for my help and advice!!! That indomitable … old woman (she was 61) is setting to work… to write it all … over again." And he chuckled at his defeat.'

And Fr Purbrick did write the Preface. He also set on record his admiration of her courage and her humility.

Love one another

In the midst of all this writing Frances was opening new convents; receiving new subjects; forming and instructing novices; planning new ventures for God. She took care of the business side, training sisters in account keeping; in wise purchasing or renting of property, and travelling to view new undertakings.

The early Sisters loved to hear Frances read and speak on the Gospel of the day. If they had to stay in bed

because of sickness, their greatest grief was that they would miss 'Mother's' instructions. One Sister wrote 'Mother would describe a scene from the Gospels vividly and repeat the words of Jesus with such deep feeling that it was usual to have all of us in tears, moved by her beautiful speaking voice, telling of the one she loved so completely.'

This spirit of prayer, her delight in slipping into the Chapel or staying on into the night hours to be with her Lord, inspired the young women more profoundly than any instructions. The first three Sisters to be professed were over twenty-five years old, almost all who came later were in their teens or early twenties. Sister Mary Elizabeth (Bathia Deverill) was a widow and a convert. She was a tower of strength to Frances and was a great listener especially when it came to the plans for spreading the love of God. The sense of the immediate presence of God in all people was an activating belief among the earliest members of the congregation. The reverence for the early call in Baptism and the reality of the indwelling of Jesus was the very foundation of all the Sisters did. It formed and coloured their life in community and it fired their work with the poor families in the Seven Dials district. This was the slum territory of many of the novels of Charles Dickens. Sister Elizabeth knew every cellar and attic and slum room filled with the poorest of London's poor. It was a crime-ridden district and even the

doctor had to have a police escort. One doctor was shocked to see Sister Elizabeth setting out on her own to visit 'her friends'. He asked a policeman why there was no escort. 'Nobody here would harm any of our Sisters, they are the friends of the poor.'

Her country childhood was the inspiration of her practical help to the slum-dwellers in Soho. She would borrow brushes and pails and go with the Sisters to show how to whitewash the rooms and so disinfect as well as clean the homes.

Fr James Cullen had, when he was still in Wexford, recommended a young woman, Margaret Doyle, to Frances as a promising subject. She was a gifted artist, intelligent and totally dedicated to the love of the Sacred Heart and of Our Blessed Lady. Her name in religion was Sister Mary Clare and she was the life and soul of the Novitiate, succeeding in everything she undertook. She loved the poor and Frances felt God had sent Clare as the one to take over the leadership of the Congregation after her. She was a clever and devoted nurse and modelled on Frances Taylor herself.

In January 1879 Frances Taylor had to travel to Rome and Mary Clare went with her as her secretary. Concern about a persistent cough was the reason for the choice of the travelling companion and the warm sunshine and the wholesome air and food did a great deal to restore Clare's health, but only for a year. She succumbed to tuberculosis,

the dreaded disease, in September. Archbishop Manning, now a Cardinal, came to see her and reminded her of the text of his homily on St Patrick's Day in Rome: 'What I do you know not now but you shall know hereafter'. Clare's deathbed was a scene of heroic sanctity; Frances Taylor slept in a small alcove and tended Clare night and day. Their deep love for the suffering Christ made it possible for both of them to accept the suffering of this painful death without a complaint. St Therese said from a similar deathbed, 'I did not know it was possible to suffer so much.'

A young promising life taken away was a deep trial of faith. Clare's own sufferings were born heroically and the community mourned her deeply. Once again, for Frances it seemed that the person likely to be her greatest help and support was taken from her. Sadly, many of the Sisters with tuberculosis, whom she nursed through their final illness, were young women in their twenties.

Among you as one who serves

Women were the main victims of poverty and too many of them ended their days in the muddy waters of the Thames. Hunger and misery forced many others to lives of crime and prostitution. It was for these women that the Poor Servants of the Mother of God set up means of employment. For unskilled people, laundry work proved to be the most successful. The women were helped back

to self-respect and to a healthy livelihood. Initially the Sisters shared the houses of refuge in the infamous Seven Dials district. As time went by larger places were more practical and employment was available for many poor women. Princes Row, Green Court, Soho were all names that caused the light to shine in the eyes of the older sisters as they remembered the joy they had in helping to fight the evils of poverty. They regaled younger generations with stories of their own adventures, going back from their visits to their little convent with tales of hungry children and sickly mothers and then being sent back with food. If there was sickness Mother Magdalen would go herself and take a young Sister with her to learn some first-hand nursing.

Frances was a person in whose presence one could not be sad or dull for long. She had an infectious laugh and carried a deep inner joy. If times were especially trying she herself would devise ways of lifting the spirits. There is a box of riddles and jokes in her own hand-writing, preserved in the Archives, every bit as precious as her spiritual writings and diaries.

One incident has always been seen as characteristic of Frances. One bitterly cold, snowy day a very poor man came asking for 'a piece of bread to bring home to his children.' He was brought in and given some hot soup but, to the surprise of the sisters, Frances put on her cloak and went out. She was back before the soup was finished,

with a large sturdy broom. This she presented to the man and asked him to brush away the snow from in front of the little Convent. When he had finished she gave him a half-crown (two shillings and sixpence, as good as a week's wages) and told him to go and earn as much as he could while the snow lasted.

Blazing blue eyes

Fr Dignam had been appointed to the mining town of St Helens, Lancashire. He was convinced that the Poor Servants could do wonders for the poor there. He could see that nurses were needed to help with the appalling injuries the men suffered in the mines. Many influential people were touched by his appeal for funds to build a hospital. Frances Taylor freed several Sisters to go and train as nurses. She naturally had to spend time in St Helens and her absence from the Sisters' refuge in Soho was noted. The Sisters were alarmed that many of the women working with them became anxious and worried while some dropped out altogether. It was discovered that the women were being threatened by their former pimps who were considerably worse off since their prey no longer earned money for them. Then the lease of the house was threatened and Frances came down from Lancashire unannounced.

Frances Taylor with her anger thoroughly aroused was a formidable person to meet. Though she was already

stout, she was so tall and still so active that her unusual size only added to her natural dignity. She was absolutely unselfconscious and fearless and to be descended upon by such a woman, her cheeks flushed with holy anger, her blue eyes blazing with righteous indignation, was no light ordeal. In this case, as in most others, she triumphed. We have no record of what happened but we may safely suppose that the threat of public exposure, made by a person of such obvious strength of purpose, was sufficient. The Sisters and the poor women of Green Court were left in peace.'

The Poor Servants of the Mother of God very soon had their constitutions approved by the Vatican, in the 'Brief of Praise' granted in 1879. In 1885 they were invited to open a convent in Rome itself. The final approval of the constitutions came in July 1900, a month after Frances Taylor's death.

'God wants to become incarnate in me'

This is the motto summarising the founding grace of Frances Taylor. Her greatest insight was that God chose to become human. She struggled with the reality of this mystery. She believed in the indwelling of God from her very Baptism and her humility delighted in the gift that all that was good in her was from God's own life within her. Her great attraction was to the mystery of the Incarnation, at the moment when Mary said 'Yes' and the

Angel departed leaving Our Lady alone, kneeling in the midst of a luminous cloud, bearing within her the Word made flesh, that moment when 'the power of the Most High did overshadow her, her hidden God hidden within her.'

Tradition has it that Mary's wish from childhood was to be the handmaid of the Lord, so Frances had the idea of calling her little group *The Servants of the Mother of God and of the Poor.* This was thought to be too long so the altered version is what was kept. The idea of the serving girl is expressed by St Ignatius in the Exercises. Frances went a step further and gave her a name. She called her '*Amata*': the loving one or the beloved. So when people made fun of the long title Frances smiled and kept silent.

The scripture uses the overshadowing cloud to convey the Spirit of God drawing close to save and protect. The cloud on Thabor overshadowed the apostles and a voice spoke, as at the Baptism, 'this is my beloved Son.' The action that followed Mary's being 'overshadowed', the Visitation, when Mary went in joy to share the Good News with her cousin Elizabeth, is the completion of prayer, the contemplative in action, the ideal for every member of the congregation. It is also the natural outcome of God's presence received into one's life. An older woman blessed by God with an unexpected pregnancy blesses the younger woman for her faith.

Mary's Magnificat is, at first, a burst of praise for God's gracious compassion in sending a Saviour. Then it soars into prophetic delight in the Lord who helps the oppressed and reverses the success of worldly arrogance.

Frances Taylor's insight into the Incarnation is before her time like so much else in her life. Her own real humanity – the way she used it as a testing ground for action, her courage to be herself and to encourage others to be fully human – is probably the most attractive aspect of her personality. Karl Rahner, a good century later than Frances, wrote:

'The first thing we should learn from Jesus is to be fully human. If the Word of God assumed a concrete existence in Jesus, then this must clearly be so great, so meaningful for the future, so full of possibilities, that God did not become anything else but a human being when he wanted to go outside of the Godhead. In Christ, God has assumed the everyday.'

And in another place,

'You see, you're actually only dealing with Jesus when you throw your arms around him and realise right down to the bottom of your being that this is still something you can still do today.'

Her love for God was obvious from her treatment of people. Sometimes she had to be stern, especially when she was trying to get the best out of her novices or young

Sisters in training. A Sister who had been give a strong reprimand would often find that later on, she was given a hot drink and an early night.

There is an extract from a letter of advice written to an inexperienced Sister who had been recently put in charge:

'About correcting a Sister, that is your duty, but when you have done so, try to show her extra kindness. For example: you have to go to London – take her as your companion so that she can visit her brother.'

She herself had an extraordinary capacity for hard work yet she was vigilant that the Sisters did not overwork: 'Give yourself time to think, don't let yourself be driven. Better leave something undone and take time to think.'

For Frances the final fifteen years of her life were spent in a Gethsemane of physical suffering: untreated diabetes being the main cause. There were convents being opened in London, Liverpool, Brighton, Paris, Rome, Dublin, and Cork. In 1899 the first workhouse in Ireland was undertaken, in Loughlinstown, County Dublin. In June 1900 she was brought to her beloved Convent in Soho critically ill. Diabetes had been diagnosed in 1894, the only treatment prescribed was to avoid overwork and worry. It was an Oblate Father, Fr Miller OMI, who gave her the last rites. He wrote:

'She was convinced it was her last illness and when I ventured to encourage her by saying that Our Lord would spare her to continue and consolidate the work the Lord had given her to do, she said: "Oh! Father, it was Our Lord who has enabled the work to subsist, and I have never been necessary; I can leave it entirely to the Lord." Her last words to the sisters round her bed were: 'Invoke the Sacred Heart'.'

Prayer for the beatification of
Frances Taylor/Mother Magdalen

Heavenly Father,
You gave to Frances Taylor/ Mother Magdalen,
a profound insight into the Mystery of the Incarnation
and a great love and compassion
for the poor and needy.
We pray that her life
of deep faith and loving service
may continue to inspire us
and that one day, she may be beatified
to the glory of your name.
We ask this through Jesus Christ Our Lord
Amen.

Major Biographies of Mother Magdalen

F.C. Devas, *Mother Magdalen Taylor* (London, 1927)

Sister Mary Campion Troughton SMG, '*Memoir of Mother Magdalen Taylor*' (1908, privately published by the Poor Servants of the Mother of God, 1972)

Mother Mary Geraldine O'Sullivan SMG, *Born to Love* (London, 1970)

Ruth Gilpin Wells, *A Woman of Her Time and Ours* (Charlotte, NC, 1988)

Sister Eithne Leonard SMG *Frances Taylor/Mother Magdalen: A Portrait* (Privately published by the Poor Servants of the Mother of God, 2005)

Some Other Sources

Poor Servants of the Mother of God, Congregational Archives:

Central Archive, St Mary's Convent, Brentford, Middlesex; Irish Regional Archive, Manor House, Raheny, Dublin

Frances Taylor, *Eastern Hospitals and English Nurses by a Lady Volunteer* (1857 edn)

Frances Taylor, *Irish Homes and Irish Hearts* (London, 1867)

Sister Angela Bolster RSM, T*he Sisters of Mercy in the Crimea War* (London, 1964)

Lambert McKenna SJ, Life and Work of Rev James Aloysius Cullen SJ (London, 1924)

Maria Luddy (ed.) *The Crimean War Journals of the Sisters of Mercy* 1854-56 (Dublin, 2004)

Sr Elizbeth Prout

Elizabeth Prout was christened as an Anglican but grew up very near to Blessed Dominic Barberi's Passionist monastery. His preaching and actions inspired her to convert to Catholicism and give her life to Christ. With the help of the Passionists Elizabeth founded an order that poor girls could join in order to bring help and education to the very poorest. Elizabeth spent the rest of her life founding convents, schools and working tirelessly for the poor in Britain. Over the last 150 years the Congregation of the Sisters of the Cross and Passion has spread all over the world and Sr Elizabeth's cause is progressing to a recognition of her heroic work.

ISBN: 978 1 86082 549 1

CTS Code: B715

Margaret Clitherow

A butcher's wife from York, Margaret was brought up in the new protestant religion, but was reconciled to the Catholic Church in 1574. Twelve years later she suffered brutal execution following years of apostolic activity, including harbouring Catholic priests. She had refused to plead at her trial in order to spare her children and servants from testifying against her. Her husband never returned to the Catholic faith, though a daughter of hers became a nun at Louvain. One of the Forty Martyrs, she was canonised in 1970.

ISBN: 978 1 86082 218 6

CTS Code: B676